Chapter 1: Birth Dates and Personality Traits: A Match Made in Heaven or a Recipe for Disaster?

The Cosmic Connection: How Your Birthday Influences Your Behavior

Ah, birthdays, the one day of the year where you can eat cake for breakfast and not feel guilty about it. But did you know that your birthday might also come with a side of personality traits? Imagine your birth date as a cosmic buffet, where each dish represents a unique characteristic that influences your behavior in business and personal relationships. So, while you're busy blowing out candles, the universe is busy handing out traits that could dictate how you navigate life, negotiations, and your friendships—talk about multitasking.

Let's dive into the zodiac signs, shall we? Each sign comes with its own quirks, strengths, and weaknesses, much like your favorite sitcom characters. If you're a fiery Aries, you might approach business deals like a bull in a china shop—enthusiastic but prone to break a few things along the way. On the other hand, our serene Libra friends might spend so much time weighing pros and cons that they'll miss the deadline entirely. Choosing partners in business or life? It's not just about compatibility; it's about avoiding the cosmic disaster that could ensue from mixing a spontaneous Sagittarius with a meticulous Capricorn.

Now, let's talk about the influence of your birth date on your communication style. Ever met someone who seems utterly incapable of receiving feedback? They might just be a stubborn Taurus, clinging to their opinions like a toddler clings to their favorite toy. In contrast, a Gemini will overanalyze every word you say, turning a simple "let's meet at noon" into a three-hour debate on the philosophical implications of time. Understanding these traits can save you from awkward conversations and help you navigate the choppy waters of business negotiations without sinking like a lead balloon.

Then there are those moments when you need to read the room—like trying to pitch a new idea to a group of skeptical Scorpios. Good luck! They'll dissect your proposal like a science project gone wrong. But if you bring in a few facts and appeal to their need for depth, you might just win them over. Similarly, knowing that a Cancer might be more comfortable in a supportive team environment can help you foster deeper connections and create a more cohesive work atmosphere. It's all about playing to the strengths of your cosmic crew.

So, the next time you're in a meeting or trying to navigate the murky waters of personal relationships, remember your birth date blueprint. Embrace the quirks that come with your zodiac sign, and be mindful of those around you. You might just discover that understanding these cosmic connections can turn potential disasters into delightful collaborations—or at the very least, give you a solid excuse for that extra slice of cake. After all, if the universe is serving up personality traits based on when you were born, you might as well enjoy the buffet!

The Zodiac Roundup: A Brief Introduction to the Stars

Welcome to "The Zodiac Roundup," where we explore the celestial circus above us and how it spills over into our everyday lives, especially in the realms of business and personal relationships. Imagine the stars as quirky characters at a cosmic cocktail party, each shining in their own unique way, and each one bringing its own brand of charm—or chaos—to your interactions. While you may not be able to see the future in the stars, you can certainly see how they influence the people you encounter, whether they're your business partners, your best friends, or that one colleague who insists on bringing tuna salad for lunch.

Now, let's be real: if you've ever tried to negotiate a deal with a stubborn Taurus, you know that their determination can match a bull charging through a china shop. And don't even get me started on the Geminis, who can flip from charming conversationalists to indecisive daydreamers faster than you can say "mercurial." The zodiac signs are not just your average astrological fluff; they are essential tools for decoding the personalities of those around you. Understanding these traits can help you navigate the tricky waters of collaboration and communication in both your business and personal lives.

Picture this: you're in a meeting, and your fiery Aries colleague is throwing out ideas like confetti. Meanwhile, the Pisces in the corner is lost in a daydream about their next vacation. By recognizing these personality traits, you can adapt your approach. Maybe you'll need to reel in the Aries' enthusiasm with some solid data, or perhaps you'll want to gently prod the Pisces back to reality with a well-timed question. Knowing these zodiac quirks allows you to tailor your strategy, making it easier to build strong working relationships.

But the fun doesn't end at the office; our zodiacal friends bring their unique flavors into our personal lives too. Imagine trying to plan a weekend getaway with your Virgo friend, who insists on creating an Excel spreadsheet detailing every minute of your itinerary. On the flip side, you might have a Sagittarius in your social circle who thinks spontaneity is a life philosophy and would rather wing it. By understanding these differences, you can harmonize your plans and ensure everyone walks away happy, rather than feeling like they just survived a family reunion gone wrong.

So, as we embark on this zodiac journey, remember that the stars have a lot to say about the people you interact with daily. Whether you're dealing with the steadfast earth signs or the unpredictable air signs, each character adds a dash of spice to your relationships. Embrace the quirks, laugh at the absurdities, and use this cosmic knowledge to enhance your connections in both business and life. And who knows? You might just find that understanding the zodiac is the secret ingredient to not only surviving but thriving in the delightful chaos of human interactions.

Can We Blame It on the Stars?

Can we really blame our quirks and foibles on the stars? If you've ever met a Taurus who refuses to budge from their favorite corner of the couch or a Gemini who can't decide whether to attend a party or stay home binge-watching their latest obsession, you might think that the cosmos is playing a cosmic joke on us. After all, what better scapegoat for our erratic behavior than the alignment of celestial bodies? "Oh, I'm sorry I snapped at you during the meeting, but have you seen Mercury? It's in retrograde!" What a convenient excuse!

Let's consider the classic case of Virgo. Known for their meticulous nature, a Virgo in the workplace can be the ultimate overthinker. If you've ever had a colleague who spends hours color-coding spreadsheets, you might suspect they were born under the sign of the Virgin. But what if that obsession with details is just a cover for some deep-seated fear of chaos? Blaming it on the stars might be easier than admitting that they have a phobia of messy desks. Next time you find yourself in a heated debate over whether the stapler belongs in the left drawer or right, remember: it's not just a personality clash; it's a celestial showdown.

Now, let's talk about the fiery Leos, whose dramatic flair can turn a simple business presentation into a full-blown Broadway show. Picture this: a Leo manager passionately gesturing about quarterly reports while the rest of the team sits with their jaws dropped, wondering if they accidentally wandered into a talent show. While it's tempting to chalk this up to astrological influence, perhaps they just really like the sound of their own voice. So, are we really taking cues from the stars, or are we just dealing with someone who's had one too many cups of coffee?

On the flip side, we've got the easy-going Libras, who can't make a decision to save their lives. If you've ever tried to plan a team lunch and found yourself asking a Libra for input, prepare for a long, winding journey through every possible cuisine. "Italian or Mexican? Well, what about Thai?" The stars might insist that Libras are all about balance, but in reality, they may just be stalling because they can't decide which Instagram filter to use for their lunch pic. Blaming it on the stars is just another way of saying, "I don't know what I want, and I'm going to make you suffer with me."

So, can we truly blame it all on the stars? Perhaps it's a little bit of both—celestial influence and our own delightful quirks. While astrology can offer some insight into our tendencies and idiosyncrasies, ultimately, we're all just trying to navigate the chaotic landscape of business and personal relationships. Whether you're a stubborn Capricorn, an indecisive Libra, or a dramatic Leo, remember that at the end of the day, we're all just humans stumbling through life, occasionally pointing fingers at the universe for a good laugh.

Chapter 2: The Twelve Signs of Business: Who's Who in the Office Zoo

Aries: The Office Rambo

Aries, the first sign of the zodiac, struts into the office like it owns the joint. If you've got an Aries in your workplace, you might as well strap on a helmet and prepare for some high-octane excitement. These are the folks who can turn a mundane meeting into a scene from an action movie, complete with dramatic pauses and an intense soundtrack. When Aries enters the room, you can almost hear the theme music swell as they announce their latest idea with the fervor of a soldier going into battle. Just remember, while they may be charging into the fray, they might also forget to check if anyone else is in the line of fire.

When it comes to decision-making, an Aries is like a bull in a china shop—if the bull were armed with a bazooka and had a flair for theatrics. They don't just make decisions; they launch them like grenades into the air, expecting everyone to jump on board. If you're on their team, be prepared for spontaneous brainstorming sessions that seem to happen at the speed of light. Sure, you might end up with a wacky plan to market office staplers as the next big thing, but at least you can count on an Aries to keep things interesting. Just make sure you carry a notepad because you might need to document the wild ride for posterity.

However, the downside of having an Aries around is that they can sometimes be a bit… overzealous. Their enthusiasm can easily turn into impatience, leaving you wondering if you're working with a motivational speaker or a drill sergeant. They have a knack for jumping headfirst into projects without stopping to consider the consequences. So, while an Aries might be busy executing their next big plan, you'll probably find yourself in the role of the reluctant voice of reason, desperately trying to ensure that no one accidentally launches the office printer into orbit.

In personal relationships, Aries brings the same fiery energy they exhibit at work. They're passionate, adventurous, and always ready to take the lead on date night—think skydiving or an impromptu road trip rather than dinner and a movie. If you can keep up with their energetic pace, you'll find an Aries makes for a thrilling partner. Just be prepared for the occasional flame-up; their tempers can ignite as quickly as their enthusiasm. Still, once the dust settles, you'll find they're quick to apologize, often with a goofy grin and a promise to cook dinner—just not a boring one, of course.

Navigating an Aries in business or personal relationships is like riding a rollercoaster. Hold on tight, enjoy the ups and downs, and prepare for unexpected twists. Their passion and drive can be infectious, pushing you to reach levels you never thought possible. Just remember to pack your sense of humor and your patience, as you'll need both to keep up with the Office Rambo. Whether you're brainstorming the next big idea or planning your next adventure, an Aries will keep you on your toes, and most importantly, make sure you're never bored.

Taurus: The Stubborn Steady

Taurus, the stubborn steady, is like that friend who insists on taking the scenic route, even when everyone else is panicking about being late. You see, Taureans are not just persistent; they're the human embodiment of a boulder rolling down a hill—slow but relentless. In business meetings, they're the ones who stay firmly rooted in their seats, arms crossed, and eyebrows furrowed, as they contemplate whether your idea is worth the effort or just another flash in the pan. If you're pitching to a Taurus, you'd better come prepared, because their famous obstinacy means they won't budge unless convinced that your proposal is as solid as their favorite brand of chocolate.

In personal relationships, a Taurus is that dependable partner who will always show up with snacks and a blanket, ready for a cozy night in. They're the type who will remember your anniversary even if you don't. But beware! Try to change their plans last minute, and you might as well be trying to move a mountain. They have a remarkable ability to dig their heels in deeper than a toddler refusing to leave the playground. So, if you're dating a Taurus, it's best to learn the art of negotiation—because suggesting a spontaneous trip to the beach instead of their beloved couch could lead to an epic showdown.

However, this stubbornness can be a double-edged sword. On one hand, their unwavering nature makes them incredibly reliable; on the other, it can lead to comical stand-offs over the most trivial matters. Picture this: a Taurus and a Gemini trying to decide on a restaurant. The Gemini suggests a trendy new spot, while the Taurus insists on their favorite old-school diner. What ensues is a delightful debate, with the Taurus firmly holding their ground, eyeing the menu of their beloved diner like it's a sacred text. In the end, the Gemini might just have to resort to bribery—perhaps an offer of dessert to sweeten the deal.

In the workplace, Taurus individuals are often the stalwarts of any team. Their dedication and work ethic make them the reliable backbone of projects. However, if they're faced with a last-minute change, don't be surprised if they exclaim, "But we had a plan!" Like an old-school GPS that refuses to recalculate, they thrive on stability and routine. Of course, their stubborn streak can lead to some humorous situations, like when they insist on sticking to a project timeline that clearly needs adjusting, while everyone else is frantically waving their arms in "emergency mode."

Ultimately, if you want to navigate the Taurus personality in both business and personal relationships, embrace their steadiness while also being prepared for their delightful stubbornness. Learn to appreciate their loyalty and the way they value tradition. Just remember, when you're brainstorming ideas or planning outings, a little patience and a sense of humor go a long way. With a Taurus, you may find yourself laughing through the debates, sharing chocolate, and enjoying the ride—just be sure to buckle up, because it's going to be a slow but steady journey.

Gemini: The Chatterbox with a Plan

Gemini, the sign of the twins, is often portrayed as the ultimate social butterfly, flitting from one conversation to another like a caffeinated hummingbird. With a mental agility that rivals the fastest internet connection, Geminis are notorious for their chatty nature. They can turn a simple "Hello" into a two-hour TED Talk, complete with plot twists and side anecdotes. If you find yourself in a meeting with a Gemini, prepare for a whirlwind of ideas, jokes, and random trivia that will likely leave you wondering how you ended up discussing the mating habits of penguins when you were supposed to be talking about quarterly projections.

But don't let the chatter fool you; beneath that playful banter lies a strategic mastermind. Geminis may seem like they're just winging it, but in reality, they've got a plan tucked away in the back of their ever-busy minds. They have an uncanny ability to read the room and adapt their ideas on the fly. One moment they're suggesting a new marketing strategy, and the next, they're whipping out their phone to illustrate their point with a meme that perfectly captures the essence of your dilemma. This blend of spontaneity and foresight makes them invaluable in both business and personal relationships, as they can pivot conversations to keep everyone engaged while steering the ship toward success.

However, this dual nature can sometimes lead to confusion. As you navigate your relationship with a Gemini, you might find yourself caught in a loop of their rapid-fire thoughts. One minute they're excited about launching a new project, and the next, they're contemplating a career as a professional kazoo player. Understanding this quirk is key; their minds are like a spinning roulette wheel, and while you might not know where it will land, the ride is sure to be entertaining. Just remember, when they start talking about their latest "brilliant" idea, it might be best to hold on tight and enjoy the ride.

Communication is the lifeblood of a Gemini's relationships. They thrive on interaction, so if you want to keep a Gemini engaged, be prepared to match their level of enthusiasm. Ask questions, share your thoughts, and don't be afraid to throw in a few witty comebacks. They appreciate a good banter, and a little playful sparring can deepen your connection. Just make sure to steer clear of topics that might lead to a serious debate—Geminis can turn a light-hearted discussion about pizza toppings into a full-blown philosophical discussion on the nature of culinary art before you know it.

In conclusion, having a Gemini in your life is like having a personal cheerleader who also moonlights as a stand-up comedian and a strategic planner. Their ability to juggle conversations while keeping an eye on the bigger picture makes them a unique asset in both business and personal settings. Embrace their chatter, engage with their ideas, and don't forget to take notes—you never know when one of their whimsical musings might spark the next big concept for your project or inspire a laugh that brightens your day. With a Gemini, every interaction is a chance to learn, laugh, and perhaps even discover a new passion for kazoo music along the way.

Cancer: The Emotional Support Colleague

When we think of a cancer in the workplace, our minds might drift to the image of an overly sensitive colleague who cries during commercials and keeps a stash of snacks hidden in their desk. But let's not underestimate the emotional support capabilities of our Cancer friends. They've mastered the art of empathy, making them the go-to for breaking down emotional barriers and offering a shoulder to cry on. Just remember, if you need to talk about your feelings, don't bring up the latest workplace drama during their lunch break; they might just shed a tear into their salad.

Cancers thrive on connections and are often the glue that holds teams together. Their ability to intuitively understand the emotional landscape of their colleagues is practically a superpower. While your other coworkers might be busy crunching numbers and meeting deadlines, the Cancer is busy ensuring that everyone feels seen and heard. They can sense when someone is having a bad day, and they'll swoop in with a comforting cup of herbal tea and a heartfelt pep talk, which can feel like a warm hug in a world full of cold emails. They might not transform into a superhero, but they certainly make the office a more compassionate place.

However, let's not forget that with great emotional support comes great emotional baggage. Cancers can sometimes take things a bit too personally, leading to a dramatic flair that would make a soap opera star proud. If you accidentally overlook their birthday, be prepared for a week of passive-aggressive post-it notes and an emotional presentation on "The Importance of Feeling Appreciated." Navigating their feelings requires a delicate touch, like walking on eggshells while juggling flaming torches. So, when they're having a moment, just remember that a little extra kindness goes a long way.

In the context of business relationships, Cancers excel at creating a nurturing environment. They're the colleagues who remember your favorite coffee order and will encourage you to take a mental health day when you're feeling overwhelmed. Their emotional intelligence helps in forging connections that can be beneficial for team dynamics and productivity. However, be sure to balance their emotional needs with your own. If you find yourself in a situation where the Cancer is having a meltdown over a spilled drink, you may need to channel your inner therapist while also making sure your deadlines aren't falling by the wayside.

Ultimately, having a Cancer on your team is like adding a fuzzy blanket to your work life—warm, comforting, and occasionally a little too clingy. They remind us that business is not just about numbers and deadlines; it's about the people behind those figures. So, the next time you find yourself with a Cancer colleague, embrace their emotional depth, share a laugh over the absurdities of office life, and appreciate the unique way they bring a sense of community to the workplace. Just don't forget to bring them a snack or two; after all, a happy Cancer is a productive Cancer.

Leo: The Office Diva

Leo, the office diva, struts into the workplace with all the flair of a Broadway star stepping onto the stage. With a mane of confidence that could rival a lion's, this zodiac sign knows how to command attention. You might find them at the water cooler regaling coworkers with tales of their weekend adventures, complete with dramatic pauses for effect. If you thought the office was a place for quiet productivity, you clearly haven't met a Leo. Their enthusiastic presence can turn even the dullest Monday morning into a lively performance—complete with spontaneous dance breaks and heartfelt monologues about their latest project.

When it comes to leadership, Leos are the ultimate showmen. They possess a natural charisma that can rally a team faster than a motivational poster can say "teamwork." However, beware of their occasional diva moments. If a Leo feels overlooked or underappreciated, you might witness a classic scene: the silent treatment combined with an exaggerated sigh. They thrive on recognition, and nothing sends them into a tailspin quite like forgetting their birthday at the office. Spoiler alert: it's a disaster waiting to happen. The cake better be triple-layer chocolate, or you'll be facing the wrath of a lion who feels they've been deprived of their rightful celebration.

In meetings, Leos are the ones who can turn a mundane agenda into a captivating spectacle. They'll pitch ideas with the flair of a seasoned actor delivering an Oscar-winning performance. Just when you think you've heard it all, they'll sprinkle in a few puns or dramatic gestures that leave the room in stitches. However, don't be surprised if they occasionally hog the spotlight. While Leos love to shine, they also have a knack for recognizing talent in others—provided it doesn't outshine their own. Sharing the limelight can be a challenge, but with the right approach, you can create a dynamic duo that brings the house down.

Despite their larger-than-life persona, Leos are fiercely loyal to their colleagues. They'll be the first to defend a team member in the face of criticism, ready to unleash their inner lioness (or lion) at a moment's notice. If you're ever feeling down, you can count on a Leo to swoop in like a superhero, complete with motivational speeches and maybe even a confetti cannon for effect. Just remember, while they adore being the center of attention, they appreciate gratitude and admiration in return. A simple "You did great" can make their day, and they will return the favor tenfold when their colleagues need that extra boost.

In personal relationships, Leos bring the same level of drama and charisma they exhibit at work. They thrive on passion and excitement, turning even the most mundane dinner date into an unforgettable experience. Just be prepared for spontaneous plans that could range from a last-minute trip to Vegas to an impromptu karaoke night. While their grand gestures and larger-than-life personality can be overwhelming at times, they also have a soft side that craves deep connections. If you can navigate the occasional diva behavior and appreciate their need for admiration, you'll find that a Leo is a loyal and vibrant companion who will keep life interesting.

Virgo: The Perfectionist with a Clipboard

Virgo, the meticulous maestro of the zodiac, enters the room armed with a clipboard, a pencil tucked behind their ear, and an unyielding dedication to order. If you've ever met a Virgo, you know that their idea of a wild night might just involve color-coding their spreadsheets while sipping herbal tea. With an eye for detail sharper than a hawk's, they can spot a typo from a mile away and will not hesitate to point it out, preferably during your presentation. You might think they have a secret life as an editor or a librarian, but no, they just can't help themselves from ensuring everything is in its rightful place.

In business relationships, a Virgo can be your greatest asset or your most relentless taskmaster. They thrive on structure and efficiency, often transforming chaotic meetings into well-organized brainstorming sessions complete with agendas and follow-up emails. If you're looking for someone to whip your team into shape, a Virgo is your go-to. Just be prepared for a barrage of questions like, "Did we really need that last donut at the meeting?" or "Are we sure that's the right font for the presentation?" Their perfectionist nature ensures that every detail is scrutinized, and while this can feel exhausting, it's also where their genius shines.

However, get ready for a little comedy show if you find yourself in a personal relationship with a Virgo. You might find them meticulously planning your weekend getaway down to the exact time to leave, how many snacks to pack, and the most efficient route to avoid traffic. It's like having a personal travel agent who also insists on bringing a first-aid kit for every possible scenario. While their intentions are pure, the level of planning might leave you wondering if spontaneity is an extinct concept in their world. Spoiler alert: it's not. They just believe that planning is the secret ingredient to fun.

Virgos often have a reputation for being overly critical, but it's really just their inner perfectionist speaking up. When they offer feedback, it's not meant to crush your spirit; it's their version of a compliment. "This is great, but have you considered using a more professional font?" is their way of saying they care about your success. So, if you can handle a little constructive criticism, you'll find that a Virgo's insights can elevate your projects to heights you never thought possible. Just remember to breathe and remind them that "good enough" exists – even if they might not agree.

At the end of the day, having a Virgo in your corner means you'll never have to worry about missing deadlines or showing up unprepared. Their commitment to excellence can be downright inspiring, even if it comes packaged with a side of anxiety over minor details. In personal and business relationships alike, embracing their quirks can lead to a delightful partnership filled with laughter, organized chaos, and a little bit of extra padding in that first-aid kit. So, the next time you encounter a Virgo, grab a clipboard, take a deep breath, and prepare to navigate the wonderful world of perfectionism.

Libra: The Diplomat in Conflict

Libra, the sign of the scales, is often portrayed as the peace-loving diplomat of the zodiac. This air sign is all about harmony, balance, and making sure everyone gets along—unless, of course, someone steals their last slice of pizza. In the world of business and personal relationships, a Libra will go to great lengths to avoid conflict, often playing the role of the mediator. They can charm the socks off a grumpy client or diffuse a heated argument between friends with the finesse of a seasoned negotiator. Just remember, while they're busy keeping the peace, they might be silently plotting a dramatic exit if things get too intense.

In the boardroom, Libras are the ones who suggest team-building exercises, even if that means a trust fall that nobody asked for. Their natural inclination towards diplomacy means they excel at understanding different perspectives, but don't be fooled—they can be as indecisive as a cat in a room full of laser pointers. When it comes to making decisions, they might weigh every option until the sun sets, leaving their colleagues wondering if they should order takeout for dinner or just starve in anticipation of the next big idea. Their quest for fairness can sometimes lead to analysis paralysis, and while they're busy contemplating the pros and cons, the rest of the team is left twiddling their thumbs.

In personal relationships, a Libra's diplomatic nature shines even brighter. They are the friends who will always listen to your woes, offer sage advice, and then manage to turn your sob story into a motivational speech—complete with a PowerPoint presentation.

However, their desire to keep the peace can sometimes lead to passive-aggressive comments that leave you scratching your head. "Oh, no, I don't mind at all that you forgot our anniversary… I just thought you had other plans!" This is where their charm can backfire, as they might avoid direct confrontation, leading to misunderstandings that could fill an entire season of a soap opera.

Yet, when the scales tip too far into the realm of conflict, a Libra can surprise you. They may appear calm and collected, but push them just a little too hard, and you'll witness a Libran transformation that rivals a superhero origin story. Suddenly, they're no longer the peaceful mediator but a fierce advocate for justice, ready to take on anyone who dares disrupt their carefully curated balance. This unexpected side can catch you off guard, making you question if you accidentally stepped on a beehive, given their surprisingly sharp tongue when provoked.

In conclusion, navigating a Libra's diplomatic tendencies can be both a delightful and challenging experience. They bring a unique flavor to business and personal relationships, blending charm with a knack for conflict resolution. Just remember to tread carefully around their scales—one wrong move, and you might find yourself in a debate about the merits of pineapple on pizza while they try to maintain the peace. Embrace the Libra's gifts, and you'll unlock a world of harmony, laughter, and the occasional unexpected showdown that keeps life interesting.

Scorpio: The Mysterious Power Player

Scorpio, the enigma of the zodiac, often struts into the room like it owns the place. With an intensity that could power a small city, Scorpios are the mysterious power players of the astrological wheel. Imagine a secret agent in a tailored suit, sipping espresso while simultaneously plotting world domination and solving the world's problems. They can be passionate, loyal, and sometimes downright intimidating, but their complex nature makes them the ultimate wild card in both business and personal relationships.

When dealing with Scorpios, it's crucial to remember they have a superpower called "persistence." They are like bulldogs with a bone—once they've sunk their teeth into a project, they won't let go until they've achieved their goal. This can be both a blessing and a curse. On one hand, you'll have a team member who will see a project through to the end, no matter the obstacles. On the other hand, you might find them obsessively redoing a report for the third time while you're still looking for the coffee machine. Scorpios thrive on challenges, and if you present them with one, be prepared for an all-out war of wits.

In personal relationships, Scorpios can be equally captivating and perplexing. They possess a magnetic charm that can draw others in, but they also have a tendency to keep their cards close to their chest. Trying to figure out what's going on in a Scorpio's mind is like trying to solve a Rubik's cube blindfolded—frustrating but oddly satisfying when you finally get it right. They value loyalty and trust above all else, but good luck getting them to open up about their feelings. It's like trying to crack a safe with an old-school lock combination. Just when you think you've got it, you realize you've been turning the dial the wrong way!

Scorpios are also notorious for their dramatic flair. When they're happy, they're over the moon, but when they're upset, it's like the end of the world. Their emotional intensity can lead to some unforgettable moments, often leaving others wondering if they just witnessed a scene from a soap opera. In business meetings, a Scorpio can go from calm and collected to passionate and fiery in the blink of an eye. Their ability to channel their emotions into their work can be incredibly motivating, but it can also make for some awkward silences if you happen to say the wrong thing.

Navigating relationships with Scorpios requires a blend of patience, humor, and a willingness to embrace the unexpected. They may come off as intimidating, but once you break through their tough exterior, you'll discover a fiercely loyal ally and a partner who will go to the ends of the earth for you. So, whether you're working on a project or trying to decode their latest mood swing, remember to keep your sense of humor handy. After all, life is too short not to enjoy the ride with a Scorpio, the mysterious power player of the zodiac.

Sagittarius: The Adventurous Idea Generator

Sagittarius, the adventurer of the zodiac, is often seen as the wild child who can't resist a good idea, even if it means packing a suitcase full of half-baked plans. If you've ever met a Sagittarius, you know they have the uncanny ability to turn a simple coffee date into an expedition to find the world's best avocado toast. With their optimistic spirit and insatiable curiosity, they can make even the most mundane tasks feel like a quest for hidden treasure. So, when you invite a Sagittarius into your business or personal life, be prepared for a whirlwind of brainstorming sessions that feel more like a carnival than a conference.

This fire sign is ruled by Jupiter, the planet of expansion and good fortune, which explains why Sagittarius individuals are natural idea generators. They have an innate ability to think outside the box—or, more accurately, outside the galaxy. You might start a meeting discussing quarterly projections, and before you know it, you're exploring the feasibility of a space tourism venture. While their grand visions can leave you scratching your head, they can also inspire you to dream bigger and push the boundaries of what's possible. Just remember to keep a close eye on the budget; they might forget to check the price tag on their latest "brilliant" scheme.

In personal relationships, a Sagittarius can be a delightful whirlwind of spontaneity and fun. They thrive on new experiences and can turn even the dullest dinner into a thrilling culinary adventure. If they suggest a last-minute road trip to a remote location, don't be surprised if you find yourself packing snacks and googling the nearest gas stations. While their adventurous spirit keeps things exciting, it can also lead to a bit of chaos, especially if you're more of a "let's plan this out" type. But hey, who needs plans when you have a Sagittarius around? Just buckle up and enjoy the ride.

However, it's important to remember that the same traits that make Sagittarius so exciting can also lead to misunderstandings. They can be blunt and overly honest, often forgetting that not everyone shares their adventurous mindset. What they see as a fun challenge might feel like a reckless leap into the unknown for others. If you're working with a Sagittarius, be ready for some spirited debates and the occasional eye roll. Their enthusiasm might come off as inconsiderate, but beneath that unfiltered exterior lies a genuine desire for everyone to enjoy life to the fullest.

In conclusion, embracing the adventurous idea generator that is Sagittarius can be both a blessing and a delightful challenge. Their infectious energy invites you to think bigger and bolder, but it also requires a dash of patience and a willingness to keep up with their whirlwind ideas. In business and personal relationships, a Sagittarius can turn routine into adventure, but it's vital to find a balance between their spontaneity and your need for structure. So, whether you're brainstorming the next big thing or simply deciding where to grab dinner, just remember: with a Sagittarius, the journey is just as important as the destination—and it's bound to be one heck of a ride!

Capricorn: The Workaholic Overachiever

Capricorns, the workaholic overachievers of the zodiac, are the kind of people who treat deadlines like a personal vendetta. If you've ever met a Capricorn, you might have noticed they have an impressive ability to turn every mundane task into a high-stakes competition. Forget about taking a leisurely stroll in the park; their idea of relaxation is crafting a PowerPoint presentation on the benefits of taking breaks. When they do take a break, it's usually to brainstorm ways to make their coffee breaks more productive.

In the workplace, Capricorns are the ones who show up early, leave late, and have a meticulously organized desk that makes Marie Kondo look like a hoarder. They thrive on order and discipline, often to the point where their colleagues suspect they might secretly be robots programmed for maximum efficiency. If there's a project deadline, you can bet your bottom dollar that the Capricorn will be the one sending out calendar invites a month in advance, complete with reminders that pop up at 2 a.m. They're not just in it to win it; they're in it to set a world record for achievement.

But it's not all spreadsheets and business plans for our dear Capricorns. Underneath that no-nonsense exterior lies a sense of humor that can catch you off guard. They might crack a joke about their overly ambitious to-do list, claiming they've scheduled time to schedule time. Their humor often surfaces as dry wit, which can be a refreshing break from their otherwise serious demeanor. Just when you think they're about to dive into another serious discussion about quarterly profits, they'll hit you with a punchline that leaves you wondering if they secretly moonlight as comedians.

In personal relationships, Capricorns can be just as intense, often treating romance like a long-term project that requires strategic planning. They approach dating like they're interviewing candidates for a high-stakes job, complete with background checks and performance reviews. If you're lucky enough to catch their eye, prepare for a relationship that's filled with goal-setting sessions and discussions about future achievements. Their partners often find themselves swept up in ambitious plans, whether it's tackling a DIY home project or planning a vacation that includes a detailed itinerary down to the minute.

Despite their work-driven nature, Capricorns are fiercely loyal and dependable friends. They might not always be the life of the party, but when the chips are down, they're the ones you can count on to show up, armed with a plan and a snack. Their love language often involves acts of service, so if you find a Capricorn taking care of your tasks while you lounge on the couch, consider yourself blessed. Just remember to appreciate their efforts with a good laugh, as they'll likely respond with a perfectly timed quip about how they're just trying to keep you from becoming a couch potato. So, when navigating relationships with a Capricorn, remember, it's all about balancing their work ethic with a dash of humor and a sprinkle of understanding.

Aquarius: The Eccentric Innovator

Aquarius, the sign of the water-bearer, is often misunderstood. Contrary to what their name might suggest, they are not pouring water but rather splashing around a cocktail of brilliance and eccentricity. Imagine having a friend who shows up to your corporate meeting wearing a tinfoil hat and discussing the merits of using telepathy in marketing strategies. That's an Aquarius for you! Their innovative ideas might seem like they're from a sci-fi movie, but that's just their way of keeping things interesting. If you're looking to spice up your business meetings, invite an Aquarius; they'll ensure no one leaves without a laugh or a new perspective on life.

In relationships, whether personal or professional, Aquarians are like fireworks—unexpected, colorful, and sometimes a little too loud for comfort. They thrive on freedom and dislike being boxed into traditional roles. If you're hoping for a predictable partner, you might want to consider a Capricorn instead. Aquarians will surprise you with their spontaneous road trips, last-minute brainstorming sessions, or even a sudden urge to start a new social initiative. Do you want to know what's even more fun? Their ideas might just work! If you can keep up with their whirlwind of creativity, you might find yourself on the cutting edge of innovation.

Now, let's talk about communication. Aquarians are known for their unique way of expressing themselves. They may drop philosophical quotes into casual conversations that leave everyone scratching their heads. "Why discuss the weather when we can ponder the existence of parallel universes?" they might say. It's essential for those in their lives to embrace this quirkiness, or else risk being left out of some truly mind-boggling discussions. The key to navigating an Aquarian's eccentricity is to engage with their ideas—no matter how wild they seem. You might find that their unique perspective can add a fresh twist to your own thinking.

However, it's not all abstract thoughts and quirky ideas. Aquarians are fiercely loyal and value their relationships deeply. They might seem aloof at times, lost in their thoughts or the latest tech gadget, but when push comes to shove, they're the ones standing up for you. They have a knack for championing causes and supporting friends in need. Just don't expect them to shower you with sappy sentiments. Their affection often comes in the form of practical support or an unexpected gift of the latest gadget they think you absolutely need—whether you do or not.

Finally, if you want to foster a successful relationship with an Aquarian, be prepared for a creative rollercoaster. They love to push boundaries and challenge the status quo. Encourage their wild ideas, and you might just find yourself embarking on adventures you never thought possible. Whether it's brainstorming new projects that defy the norm or simply enjoying a night of unconventional fun, they'll keep you on your toes. Embrace their eccentricities, and you'll not only survive but thrive alongside this innovative sign. Remember, life with an Aquarius is never dull—it's an exhilarating ride full of surprises!

Pisces: The Dreamy Creative

Pisces, the twelfth sign of the zodiac, is often likened to a whimsical fish swimming in the deep ocean of dreams and creativity. If you have a Pisces in your life, you may have noticed their unique ability to turn the mundane into the magical. These folks have a knack for daydreaming, often getting lost in their thoughts, making them the perfect candidates for creative endeavors. However, if you're trying to have a serious business meeting, you might want to bring a life raft; otherwise, you may find yourself floating away on a sea of their fantastical ideas.

One moment, your Pisces friend could be brainstorming the next big app that helps cats communicate with their owners, and the next, they'll be pondering the existential crisis of a sandwich. It's a wild ride, and while their ideas might seem a bit out there, they often have a kernel of brilliance hidden within. In business, this means you can expect the unexpected—sometimes leading to innovative solutions that your more practical-minded colleagues may overlook. Just keep a notepad handy to capture their flow of thoughts before they swim off into the next abstract idea about the moon's influence on pizza toppings.

When it comes to relationships, Pisces can be incredibly empathetic, making them the perfect confidant. They have an innate ability to sense the emotions of others, which can be both a blessing and a curse. On the plus side, they'll remember your birthday and exactly how you felt on that day, but on the downside, they might also be the ones who text you at 3 a.m. asking if you're okay because they had a dream about you being chased by a giant marshmallow. Navigating these emotional waters can be tricky, but if you can handle their occasional whimsical detours, you'll find a loyal and understanding partner.

However, it's important to recognize that Pisces can sometimes get a bit lost in their own dreamy world. In business, this can lead to procrastination or indecision, especially when they're faced with choices that lack a clear emotional angle. If you're working with a

Pisces, try to bring them back to reality with concrete deadlines or the promise of snacks as a reward for completing tasks. A little structure can go a long way in helping them channel their creativity into productive outcomes, rather than allowing their vivid imagination to derail the project.

In conclusion, if you're looking to cultivate a fruitful relationship with a Pisces, embrace their creativity and emotional depth while providing a sprinkle of grounding reality. They may be the dreamers of the zodiac, but with the right balance, they can help you turn those dreams into achievable goals. So, whether you're collaborating on a business venture or navigating personal relationships, just remember to keep a fishing net handy—because you never know when a brilliant idea might just swim by, and you'll want to catch it before it disappears into the depths of their imagination.

Chapter 3: Zodiac Signs in the Boardroom: Negotiation or Nonsense?

Reading the Room: How to Spot Your Opponent's Sign

In the world of business and personal relationships, reading the room is as essential as knowing when to offer a slice of cake at a meeting. You might think you're just standing there, nodding along, but underneath that professional facade, everyone is buzzing with thoughts that could make or break a deal. So, how do you tap into this secret language? Well, it starts with spotting your opponent's signs—no, not the ones that tell you where to park. We're talking about the subtle cues that reveal their true feelings, intentions, and maybe even that they just had a questionable lunch.

First off, let's talk about body language. If your opponent is leaning back in their chair, arms crossed like they're guarding the last piece of chocolate at a family gathering, it's a clear sign they might be feeling defensive or closed off. On the flip side, if they're leaning forward, eyes wide like a kid in a candy store, they're likely interested—or they just spotted a particularly delicious donut on the table. Remember, though, reading body language is a bit like reading a menu in a foreign language; it takes practice, and you might end up ordering something you didn't intend to.

Next, let's turn our attention to mirroring. If you notice your opponent suddenly adopting your posture, you've either struck a chord or they've been secretly taking notes on how to become you. It's a classic psychological trick, and if they start mirroring your expressions, congratulations! You've officially entered the realm of rapport. But beware! If they mimic your eye roll when the boss mentions "synergy," it might just mean you've found a kindred spirit—or someone who shares your disdain for corporate jargon.

Vocal tone is another sneaky sign to consider. If their voice goes up an octave when discussing a topic, they might either be excited or just had a strong cup of coffee. Conversely, if their tone drops and becomes monotone, it's a signal to pay attention—they might be bored or plotting their escape route. The key is to tune in to these vocal cues like a seasoned detective. You'll soon find that decoding the highs and lows of conversation can be more revealing than a reality TV show finale.

Lastly, let's not underestimate the power of silence. When the conversation hits a lull and your opponent suddenly resembles a deer caught in headlights, it could mean they're weighing their options, or the last few seconds of awkward silence have made them question their life choices. Use this time wisely! A well-timed question can either drag them back into the conversation or lead them to reveal more than they intended. So, keep your ears perked and your eyes peeled; the next time you find yourself in a meeting, remember: reading the room is less about being a psychic and more about being a savvy observer with a dash of humor.

The Art of Negotiation: Using Astrology to Get Your Way

Negotiation can often feel like a game of chess, where one misstep can send your carefully crafted strategy spiraling into chaos. But what if I told you that the stars could be your secret weapon? Yep, you heard that right! Forget about conventional negotiation tactics; let's dive into the cosmic realm and explore how astrology can help you charm your way to victory in both business and personal relationships. Picture this: instead of just addressing your counterpart's needs, you align your pitch with their zodiac traits. It's like finding the cheat code for human interaction!

Let's start with the fiery Aries. If you're negotiating with an Aries, be prepared for a whirlwind of enthusiasm and impatience. They want results, and they want them yesterday! So, when you're presenting your proposal, drop in some high-energy phrases and a sense of urgency. Think of it like feeding a toddler a candy bar—quick, flashy, and oh-so-tempting! Just remember, if you sense that they're ready to charge ahead without considering your point of view, calmly remind them that the best deals are a marathon, not a sprint. Who knew that a bit of astrological wisdom could turn your negotiations into a relay race?

Now, let's talk about the patient and practical Taurus. If you're facing a Taurus in negotiations, you might as well prepare for a slow-cooked meal instead of a microwave dinner. They appreciate quality and durability, so when you pitch your ideas, highlight the long-term benefits and stability of your proposal. Just avoid any vague promises; Taurus folks can smell an empty sales pitch from a mile away. They'll patiently weigh their options, so it's best to come armed with facts and figures. And don't be surprised if they pull out a snack mid-meeting; they may be negotiating, but they also believe in keeping their energy levels up!

When it comes to the air signs like Gemini and Libra, you've got to keep your wits about you. Gemini thrives on conversation, so make your pitch a dialogue rather than a monologue. They love to bounce ideas around, so welcome their input as if you've just stumbled upon a hidden treasure. Meanwhile, Libras are the social butterflies who can't stand conflict, so play the diplomat. Use phrases like "We can both win here" or "Let's find a solution that works for everyone." Charm them with your charisma, and you might just walk away with a deal sweeter than honey. Just be aware that if negotiation turns into a debate, you may find yourself debating the merits of pineapple on pizza—an entirely different negotiation altogether!

Finally, let's not forget about the analytical earth signs like Virgo and Capricorn. These folks are the pragmatists who love to dig into the details. If you're negotiating with a Virgo, prepare to have your data organized and your arguments well-articulated. They have a knack for spotting flaws, so make sure you've ironed out the kinks in your pitch. With Capricorns, it's all about respect and authority. Show them you mean business by coming prepared and demonstrating your expertise. But here's the twist: while they may seem all business, don't forget to sprinkle in a little humor. After all, who says negotiations can't be a good laugh? Just make sure it's the right kind of humor; you wouldn't want to be the punchline!

So, the next time you find yourself staring down the barrel of a negotiation, look to the stars for guidance. By understanding your counterpart's zodiac traits, you can tailor your approach and increase your chances of success. Whether you're dealing with a fiery Aries or a grounded Capricorn, keeping it cosmic may just lead to a win-win situation. After all, why leave your fate to chance when the universe is willing to lend a hand—or a star?

When Signs Collide: Conflict Resolution Based on Birth Dates

When it comes to navigating the treacherous waters of personal and business relationships, knowing someone's birth date can feel like wielding a magical wand—or a ticking time bomb. Picture this: you're in a meeting with a Leo who thinks they are the rightful king of the office jungle, while a Virgo, armed with spreadsheets and an eye for detail, is trying to keep the peace. The clash of fiery ambition and meticulous planning can lead to more drama than a reality TV show. But fear not! Understanding these astrological quirks can turn potential conflicts into comedic gold.

Let's dive into the zodiac soup where signs collide like two cars at a stoplight. Aries, always eager to take the lead, can often run headlong into a sensitive Cancer who's just trying to keep their shell intact. The result? An awkward silence that feels like an eternity, followed by an emotional outburst that makes the office coffee machine seem less intimidating. If only Aries knew that Cancers require a little more nurturing than a one-liner and a high-five. This is where humor comes in. A light-hearted joke about how Aries should take a "chill pill" can lighten the mood and pave the way for understanding.

Now, let's not forget the Gemini twins. You can't trust them to stay on one topic for too long. One moment they're discussing quarterly reports, and the next, they're planning a vacation to Mars. This can drive a single-minded Capricorn up the wall. While Capricorn is busy calculating profit margins, Gemini is daydreaming about intergalactic adventures. To resolve this, Capricorn might just need to accept that sometimes, the best ideas come from those who aren't chained to their desks. Throw in a clever pun about "out-of-this-world ideas," and you'll find a way to merge practicality with whimsy.

Of course, there's the classic Scorpio and Sagittarius showdown. Scorpios are the emotional detectives, while Sagittarians are the free spirits, running around like they just won the lottery. When Scorpio's probing questions meet Sagittarius's aversion to anything resembling a commitment, it's like watching a cat try to catch a laser pointer. The key here is to embrace the chaos with laughter. A well-timed quip about "Scorpio being the detective in a comedy show" can remind everyone to take a step back and see the absurdity of their own reactions.

Finally, let's wrap it up with this: understanding birth dates and the associated personality traits is not just about avoiding drama—it's about embracing the quirks that make each zodiac sign unique. Instead of viewing conflicts as obstacles, why not see them as opportunities for laughter and growth? When signs collide, a little humor can go a long way, transforming potential clashes into moments of connection. After all, if you can learn to laugh together, you can conquer the world—or at least the next big business deal.

Chapter 4: Building Relationships: The Stars Align (or Not)

The Perfect Match: Who's Your Zodiac Bestie?

Let's face it, finding your perfect match in the zodiac realm is a bit like dating in the digital age: swiping left, right, and possibly getting ghosted by your own birth chart. But fear not, because your zodiac bestie is out there, and they are ready to bring some cosmic joy to your life! Whether you're looking for a partner in business or a confidant for your personal escapades, the stars have some stellar recommendations based on your sun sign. So, grab your astrological coffee and let's dive into the celestial matchmaking game.

Aries, the trailblazer of the zodiac, thrives on excitement and adventure. Your bestie? A fellow fire sign, Leo, who is always up for spontaneous road trips and competitive gaming sessions. Just be prepared for some friendly rivalry—when you both decide to race to the finish line, it's less "may the best person win" and more "may the best fire sign win." Meanwhile, the calm and collected Taurus will find their best match in the nurturing Cancer. Together, you'll create a sanctuary of snacks and Netflix, discussing how to make the perfect guacamole while secretly judging everyone who doesn't appreciate the art of a good avocado.

Gemini, the social butterfly of the zodiac, is best paired with the free-spirited Sagittarius. This duo can take on the world, one spontaneous party at a time. Just remember, communication is key—Gemini loves to talk, and Sagittarius loves to philosophize, which can lead to hours of deep, meaningful conversations about whether pizza is more of a pie or a flatbread. For the grounded Virgo, the perfect bestie is none other than the loyal Capricorn. You two can bond over spreadsheets and to-do lists, creating an empire of efficiency and practicality while simultaneously plotting world domination through well-structured plans.

Now, let's not forget about the water signs! Scorpio's intensity finds its match in the imaginative Pisces. Together, you'll explore the depths of emotion, but beware of the drama! One minute you're discussing your dreams, and the next you're in a full-blown soap opera. Meanwhile, the easy-going Libra will vibe best with the charming Aquarius. This duo will dazzle at social gatherings, effortlessly making new friends while spreading their unique brand of charm and wit. Just be careful not to get too lost in conversation; you might forget to actually eat that delicious cheese platter!

Finally, it's all about finding balance. Each zodiac sign has its quirks and charms that can either complement or clash with others. Just remember, relationships—whether business or personal—are a dance. Sometimes you lead, sometimes you follow, and occasionally, you step on each other's toes. Embrace the quirks of your zodiac bestie, and you'll find that navigating life's challenges is a lot more fun when you've got a cosmic companion by your side. So, who's your zodiac bestie? Let the stars guide you as you embark on this humorous journey of friendship and collaboration!

The "No Way" Factor: Signs That Clash

In the colorful world of personality traits, one of the most entertaining challenges is deciphering the "No Way" factor. This is the unmistakable vibe you get when two personalities clash like titans in a toddler's playground. Think of it as the universe's way of giving you a giant neon sign that says, "Maybe you should rethink that partnership!" It's like a cosmic game of dodgeball, where instead of balls, you're dodging awkward conversations and questionable decisions. If you've ever found yourself in a meeting where the air is so thick with tension you could cut it with a butter knife, then congratulations! You've just experienced the "No Way" factor firsthand.

First up on the list of signs that clash is the infamous "Opposites Attract" theory. Sure, it sounds romantic in theory, like a movie where the nerdy librarian and the rebellious rock star fall in love. But in the realm of business and personal relationships, it often leads to chaos. Imagine a meticulous Virgo trying to collaborate with a free-spirited Sagittarius. The Virgo has spreadsheets and Gantt charts, while the Sagittarius is busy planning their next spontaneous trip to Vegas. The result? A lot of frustrated sighs and the Virgo muttering under their breath about how they can't have a meeting without an agenda. Spoiler alert: The agenda is definitely going to get tossed out the window!

Next up, we have the "Communication Breakdown" sign. If you find yourself speaking in different languages—figuratively, of course—you might be in a "No Way" situation. Take a classic Capricorn and a chatty Gemini. The Capricorn is all about serious business, while the Gemini is spinning tales that would make even the best novelists envious. When the Capricorn wants to discuss quarterly projections, the Gemini is still on last weekend's escapades. Cue the eye rolls and the internal monologues that go something like, "Why on earth did I think this was a good idea?" If you're not careful, you might just end up in a perpetual loop of misunderstandings, where every conversation is a game of telephone gone wrong.

Then there's the "Power Struggle" sign, which is like watching a battle royale unfold in the office. Picture two Leos trying to claim the title of "Top Dog." It's all fun and games until someone realizes they're both fiercely competitive and neither is willing to back down. The boardroom becomes a coliseum, and you, my friend, are just trying to find a safe corner to sip your coffee. If you ever find yourself thinking, "Why did I sign up for this circus?" you've officially entered the realm of the "No Way" factor. The lesson here? Sometimes it's better to let someone else wear the crown—unless you're ready for a royal rumble.

Finally, we can't ignore the dreaded "Emotional Rollercoaster" sign. If your relationship feels like a soap opera where every day brings new levels of drama, you might be in trouble. Picture a sensitive Cancer paired with a nonchalant Aquarius. The Cancer is pouring their heart out while the Aquarius is nodding along as if they're listening to elevator music. This mismatch can lead to emotional confusion, with one party feeling like they're running a marathon while the other is leisurely strolling through a park. If you ever find yourself wondering why your conversations resemble a telenovela, it's time to reassess whether this partnership is truly meant to be, or if it's just the universe's idea of a practical joke.

Lessons from the Cosmos: How to Communicate with Any Sign

Ever find yourself staring at the stars, wondering if the universe is trying to send you a message? Spoiler alert: it probably is! The cosmos has been communicating with us since the dawn of time, and understanding how to decode those celestial signals can be your secret weapon in both business and personal relationships. Whether you're trying to negotiate a deal or figure out why your friend keeps texting you at 3 a.m., learning the cosmic language of zodiac signs can turn those awkward moments into cosmic connections.

First off, let's address the elephant in the room: astrology isn't just for your quirky aunt with the crystal collection. Each zodiac sign is like a personality cheat sheet, giving you insights into how people tick. For instance, if you're dealing with a fiery Aries, prepare for a high-energy interaction that could either lead to a groundbreaking idea or a spontaneous dance party. On the other hand, approach a moody Cancer with caution; one wrong word could send them into a shell that would make a hermit crab look social. Knowing these traits can save you from stepping on toes or, worse, crushing egos.

Now, you might be wondering how this cosmic knowledge can help you in the boardroom. Have you ever tried to convince a stubborn Capricorn to change their mind? Good luck! These folks are as steadfast as a mountain goat and just as stubborn. Instead of pushing against their rocky demeanor, use their practicality to your advantage. Present your ideas with solid facts and figures, and watch them nod along like they've just discovered the secret to the universe. Suddenly, you're not just a colleague; you're a trusted advisor, thanks to a little celestial guidance.

Let's not forget about the social butterflies of the zodiac—the Geminis. If you're in a meeting with a Gemini, buckle up for a whirlwind of ideas, banter, and possibly a rabbit hole or two. They thrive on communication, so throw in some humor and watch them light up like a Christmas tree. But beware: if you don't keep up, they might just take off, leaving you wondering what happened to your original agenda. It's a delicate balance, but once you get the hang of it, you'll be the star of the show—or at least the meeting.

Finally, remember that every sign has its quirks and charms. Learning to communicate effectively with each one is like mastering a new language. Sure, you might fumble over a few words or misinterpret a sign now and then, but that's all part of the cosmic comedy. The key is to embrace the differences and find the humor in the process. After all, whether you're navigating the complexities of a business deal or the mysteries of a friendship, a little laughter can go a long way. So, the next time you look up at the night sky, just remember: the universe isn't just watching; it's whispering the secrets to better relationships in your ear.

Chapter 5: Love in the Workplace: Is It Written in the Stars?

Office Romances: A Match Made in HR's Nightmare

Office romances are the delightful chaos that can make HR's hair turn gray faster than a double espresso on a Monday morning. Picture this: two star-crossed lovers, passionately stealing glances over the copy machine, while the office cat-eyeing gossip mill churns out fresh rumors like clockwork. What's not to love? The thrill of sneaking away for a quick coffee date in the break room, the excitement of shared elevator rides, and those awkward "Did we just bump into each other?" moments that make even the most stoic of colleagues crack a smile. But let's not forget, behind the romantic spark lies a minefield of HR policies and the potential for drama that could rival a daytime soap opera.

When it comes to love in the workplace, the zodiac signs could play a starring role in this romantic comedy. Imagine an Aries charging in with confidence, while the sensitive Cancer tries to figure out if their crush is just being friendly or if there's something more behind that lingering look during the morning team meeting. You can bet the office rumor mill will have a field day with it. Meanwhile, the pragmatic Virgo is over there taking notes, ensuring every flirtation is appropriately documented in case it needs to be reviewed during the annual performance evaluations. Who knew that dating someone who shares a cubicle could lead to such a thrilling blend of romance and paperwork?

Of course, let's not overlook the distinct personalities that can lead to some truly hilarious scenarios. The free-spirited Sagittarius might be all for love in the workplace, while the serious Capricorn is calculating the odds of a breakup affecting their career trajectory. Can you imagine the conversations these two would have over lunch? "So, when we inevitably break up, will we still be able to share the same coffee machine, or do I need to switch my caffeine source?" Nothing says "professionalism" quite like a couple navigating the complexities of love while trying to avoid eye contact during team meetings.

And as much as we love a good office romance story, the reality is that it often comes with a side of complications. What happens when the passionate Leo and the aloof Aquarius find themselves in a love triangle with the unsuspecting intern? Cue the awkward team-building exercises and questionable "trust falls" that could leave everyone wondering if they should trust their coworkers or just avoid eye contact altogether. It's a classic case of "will they, won't they," but in the office, the stakes can feel much higher—especially when you're worried about who's going to spill the beans to HR first.

At the end of the day, office romances are a wild ride that blends love, laughter, and a healthy dose of chaos. If you find yourself swept up in the charm of a workplace relationship, just remember to keep the HR handbook close and your sense of humor closer. After all, navigating the personalities involved can be just as important as the relationship itself. With the right mix of communication, understanding zodiac quirks, and perhaps a pinch of discretion, you might just turn what could be HR's nightmare into a beautiful love story—complete with a few laugh-out-loud moments along the way.

The Dos and Don'ts of Zodiac Dating at Work

When it comes to zodiac dating in the office, there are a few dos and don'ts that can turn your mundane work environment into a cosmic love fest—or a complete disaster. First and foremost, do embrace the charm of your astrological sign, but don't go overboard. Sure, your fellow Aries might be competitive and eager for a thrilling office romance, but that doesn't mean you should challenge them to a race to the coffee machine. This is the workplace, not a celestial version of Survivor. Keep it light-hearted, and remember, no one wants to be the subject of an office gossip column because you took a "friendly" wager a little too seriously.

Next up, do use your zodiac knowledge as a fun icebreaker to spark conversations. If you discover that your crush is a Leo, feel free to compliment their radiant energy. Just don't make it a full-blown astrological analysis at the water cooler. "Hey, I noticed you're a Leo. Did you know that means you're destined to be the center of attention?" might sound charming, but it could also come off as a little creepy. Keep it casual and avoid sounding like the office's resident horoscopist. It's all about balance—enjoy the connection without turning every interaction into an astrological lecture.

Now, let's talk about boundaries. Do respect the personal space of your colleagues, regardless of their zodiac sign. While a Scorpio might appreciate a little mystery, they definitely don't want you lurking in the shadows, waiting for the perfect moment to strike up a conversation. No one likes a workplace stalker, even if you think you're channeling your inner romantic. So, keep those boundaries clear—flirt a little, but don't turn the break room into your personal love nest. And if you sense that your flirtations are met with cold stares, it's probably a sign (pun intended) to back off.

When it comes to office outings, do consider planning events around the zodiac calendar. A themed party that celebrates each sign can be a fantastic way to foster connections without any awkwardness. However, don't use these gatherings as a platform for your one-sided crush. No one wants to be cornered at the Aquarius-themed cocktail hour while you wax poetic about their dreamy traits. Keep the vibes positive and inclusive—everyone should feel like they can mingle without being put on the spot. Save the heavy flirting for after hours or off-site, where the only office politics are who gets to choose the karaoke song.

Lastly, do remember that everyone's zodiac sign is just one slice of the personality pie. Don't let it become the sole factor in your dating endeavors. If you're a Capricorn and find yourself smitten with a free-spirited Sagittarius, embrace the differences! But don't roll your eyes when they suggest a spontaneous lunch outing instead of sticking to the rigid schedule you've meticulously crafted. Flexibility is key! So, as you navigate the starry waters of workplace romance, keep your humor intact, your mind open, and, most importantly, your office mates entertained rather than bewildered by your astrological antics.

Breaking Up: How Your Sign Reacts to Workplace Drama

When workplace drama hits, it's like a reality TV show in the office, and your zodiac sign is the quirky character stealing the spotlight. Aries, the fiery ram, charges in headfirst, often creating more chaos than they solve. They tackle drama with the enthusiasm of a toddler in a candy store, shouting, "Let's fix this!" But more often than not, they end up igniting a full-blown office war. The other signs watch in amazement as Aries throws caution to the wind, proving once again that not all heroes wear capes—some just wear a headset and a very serious expression.

Taurus, on the other hand, takes a more leisurely approach to workplace drama. While everyone else is in a frenzy, Taurus is quietly munching on a snack, contemplating the best way to respond. They believe in the power of stability and often opt for the "let's all just chill" strategy. When confronted with gossip, Taurus will likely respond with a nonchalant shrug and a reminder that it's lunchtime somewhere. Their motto? "Why fight when you can eat?" They have an uncanny ability to diffuse tensions simply by suggesting a snack break.

Gemini, the social butterfly, thrives on the buzz of office drama. They're the first to jump into the fray, armed with witty comebacks and enough gossip to fuel a soap opera. Their reaction is like a live tweet of the latest office scandal, complete with emojis. If drama were a sport, Gemini would be the star athlete, spinning tales and rallying support with the charm of a seasoned politician. But beware—once the drama dies down, they may just flit away to the next exciting distraction, leaving the aftermath for others to clean up.

Cancer feels the emotional weight of workplace drama like a sponge in a rainstorm. They approach conflicts with all the sensitivity of a concerned mother hen, often turning the drama into a heartfelt group therapy session. Expect lots of hugs, tissue boxes, and maybe even a few tears. Cancers are known for their nurturing nature, and they will try to mend hurt feelings with homemade cookies or a heartfelt chat over coffee. They believe that every conflict can be resolved with a good cry and a plate of baked goods, creating a cozy yet slightly overwhelming atmosphere.

Finally, we have Leo, the grand maestro of workplace drama. Leo doesn't just react; they perform. When drama unfolds, they see it as their stage to shine. They'll strut into the room, ready to take charge with all the flair of a Broadway star. "Let me handle this!" they declare, flashing their confident smile. For Leo, every piece of gossip is an opportunity to showcase their leadership skills, often leaving others wondering if they just witnessed a team meeting or an award-winning monologue. They may not always resolve the issue, but they'll certainly ensure everyone knows they were involved, resulting in a grand spectacle that no one will forget.

Chapter 6: Personal Growth: Becoming the Best Version of Your Zodiac Self

The Power of Self-Awareness: Know Thy Sign

Self-awareness is like having a personal GPS for navigating the wild terrain of business and personal relationships. Imagine driving through life without knowing where you're headed or what kind of vehicle you're in. You might think you're cruising in a sleek sports car, only to realize you're actually in a clunky old minivan filled with half-eaten snacks and questionable air fresheners. Knowing your birth date and the zodiac sign it corresponds to can help you tune in to your own quirks, strengths, and, let's face it, delightful shortcomings. It's time to embrace your inner astrologer and figure out what the stars were trying to tell you when you popped into the world.

Let's kick things off with the fire signs: Aries, Leo, and Sagittarius. If you're one of these fiery folks, you probably know you're a natural-born leader and the life of the party. You may also have a tendency to charge into situations headfirst, leaving a trail of chaos behind you. Self-awareness helps you realize that while your enthusiasm can be contagious, it can also incinerate a few bridges along the way. Learning to temper that fiery spirit with some patience and consideration for others can turn you from a reckless ram into a wise old sage—well, at least until the next time you get an idea that sounds too good to be true.

Next up are the earth signs: Taurus, Virgo, and Capricorn. These grounded individuals often have their feet firmly planted on the ground, which is great unless you accidentally step on a metaphorical rake and get smacked in the face with your own stubbornness. Self-awareness can help you navigate the rocky terrain of relationships by recognizing when you need to budge a little. Sure, you love stability and routine, but sometimes you've got to be willing to shake things up a bit. Just think of it as a dance-off with your inner self—sometimes you just need to let loose and bust a move instead of standing there like a statue contemplating the meaning of life.

Then we have the air signs: Gemini, Libra, and Aquarius. If you find yourself flitting from one idea to another faster than a squirrel on espresso, you might be one of these air sign adventurers. Your charm and wit can light up a room, but your tendency to overthink everything can leave you paralyzed at the crossroads of indecision. Self-awareness allows you to recognize when you're caught in a whirlwind of thoughts and helps you ground those ideas into actionable plans. After all, you can't just float around in the clouds forever; eventually, you've got to land and make something happen—preferably without crashing into a tree.

Last but certainly not least, we have the water signs: Cancer, Scorpio, and Pisces. If you've ever found yourself crying at a commercial or feeling every emotion in the room like a sponge, congratulations, you're a water sign! Your depth of feeling is a gift, but it can also feel like a double-edged sword. Self-awareness helps you understand when to dive deep into your emotions and when to float above the surface for a little bit of perspective. Remember, not every situation requires a full-blown emotional tidal wave. Sometimes a gentle splash will do, and you'll find that your relationships become smoother and more enjoyable when you don't make every conversation a dramatic soap opera episode. Embrace your sign, know thyself, and watch as the magic unfolds in your business and personal relationships.

Using Astrology for Personal Development

Astrology often gets a bad rap as the mystical realm of starry-eyed romantics, but let's take a moment to acknowledge the cosmic genius behind it. Think of astrology as the universe's very own personality test, with a side of cosmic humor. Your birth date is not just a random lottery number; it's like the universe's way of giving you a personality blueprint. So, the next time someone asks why you're so stubborn, just blame it on the stars. They set you up for greatness—or at least for some entertaining dinner conversations.

Imagine walking into a meeting full of people who have no clue that their birth signs are secretly guiding their behavior. The Aries is probably leading the charge, while the Pisces is in the corner, daydreaming about a more serene ocean view. Understanding these dynamics can be a game changer in business and personal relationships. By learning about zodiac signs, you can navigate the labyrinth of human interactions with the grace of a cat on a hot tin roof. Sure, you might not convert everyone into astrology enthusiasts, but knowing your colleague is a Scorpio may just save you from a surprise meltdown in the break room.

Now, you might be thinking, "I can barely remember my own birthday, let alone everyone else's zodiac sign!" Fear not, because astrology is less about memorizing charts and more about recognizing patterns. Just like you wouldn't wear socks with sandals (unless you're trying to make a statement), you can learn to recognize the traits associated with each sign and how they mesh—or clash—with yours. This knowledge can help you avoid stepping on any metaphorical toes and create a more harmonious work environment, or at least keep the coffee pot from becoming a battlefield.

In our quest for personal development, astrology provides us with a mirror—albeit a slightly warped one—reflecting our strengths and weaknesses. That Leo coworker who always needs attention? They're not just being dramatic; they're fulfilling their cosmic role. By embracing these traits rather than battling against them, you can channel that fiery energy into something productive, like brainstorming new ideas instead of just fighting over who gets to choose the music playlist. After all, every zodiac sign has its quirks, and understanding them can help us laugh rather than cringe.

So, the next time you find yourself in a sticky situation, remember that astrology can be your trusty sidekick. It's like having a personalized instruction manual for each person in your life—complete with quirky anecdotes and cosmic jokes. By using these insights for personal development, you can foster relationships that are not only effective but also hilariously entertaining. Who knew that the secret to navigating the complexities of business and personal relationships was just a few star alignments away? Now, go forth and embrace your astrological destiny—just don't forget to check your daily horoscope first!

The Future is Now: Setting Goals Based on Your Birth Date

Setting goals based on your birth date might sound like something your horoscope-loving aunt would suggest over brunch, but hear me out! Imagine your birth date as a cosmic GPS, guiding you through the sometimes murky waters of business and personal relationships. Picture it: every time you look at your calendar, instead of just seeing deadlines and birthdays, you see a roadmap to your best self. So, let's take a lighthearted dive into how your special day can help you set goals that are as unique as you are—without the need for a crystal ball or a tarot card reading.

First things first, let's talk about those numbers. Your birth date isn't just a random collection of digits that your parents scribbled on a birth certificate; it's a treasure trove of personality traits and potential. Think of it like a quirky cocktail: your day, month, and year combine to create a unique flavor profile that influences how you interact with the world. Want to be a better leader? Maybe your birth date suggests you should embrace that fiery nature and take risks. Or perhaps you should channel your inner introvert and focus on building one-on-one relationships. Either way, your birth date is your secret weapon in the battle of goal-setting!

Now, let's sprinkle in some zodiac magic. If you're feeling a bit lost, why not consult the stars? Your zodiac sign can add an extra layer of insight into your goal-setting strategy. Are you a fiery Aries, charging headfirst into challenges? Set some audacious goals that would make any daredevil proud. Or perhaps you're a sensitive Cancer, preferring to nurture relationships over ruffling feathers. Your goals might involve creating a supportive team environment. And if you're a whimsical Aquarius, don't be afraid to throw in some unconventional aspirations to spice things up. After all, who says your goals can't include starting a business that sells artisanal socks?

Let's not forget the importance of accountability—because, let's be honest, we all need a push sometimes. Share your birth date-based goals with friends, family, or even colleagues. You'd be surprised how much motivation a little friendly competition can provide. "Oh, you're trying to be more assertive because you're a Leo? Well, watch out world, I'm a Capricorn with a plan!" Collaborative goal-setting can transform your journey from a solitary trek into a hilarious road trip filled with unexpected detours and karaoke sessions. Who knew personal development could come with such a fantastic soundtrack?

Finally, as you embrace your birth date as a tool for goal-setting, remember to keep it fun. Life's too short to take everything seriously. If you find yourself stressed over achieving that ambitious goal, just laugh it off. After all, you're not just a product of your birth date; you're a unique individual with dreams and quirks that make you, well, you! Use your birth date as a jumping-off point, but don't forget to add your own flair. Goals should be a reflection of who you are, so let your personality shine through, even if that means occasionally veering off the beaten path in pursuit of something delightfully unexpected!

Chapter 7: The Astrological Toolbox: Tips and Tricks for Navigating Life

Daily Horoscopes: A Guide to Surviving the Week

Daily horoscopes can feel like that quirky coworker who brings donuts to the office but also insists on telling you about their cat's dreams. They're entertaining, sometimes baffling, and often leave you wondering if you should really take advice from the stars or just stick to your morning coffee. But fear not, for the celestial guides can actually be quite useful in navigating your week, especially when it comes to business and personal relationships. Whether you're a fiery Aries or a laid-back Pisces, your horoscope can provide the kind of insight that makes you feel like you've got a cosmic cheat sheet for the week ahead.

Aries, my go-getter friend, your horoscope is practically screaming at you to take charge this week. The stars are aligned for you to strut into the office like you own the place. Just remember, while confidence is key, there's a fine line between being assertive and being a bull in a china shop. Try not to scare off your colleagues, or they may start hiding their staplers and pretending to be busy whenever you walk by. A little charm can go a long way, so sprinkle in some grace with that fiery determination.

Taurus, it's time to channel your inner zen master. Your weekly horoscope suggests that harmony is essential in your personal relationships. So, if your partner suggests a quiet night in, don't roll your eyes like you just heard the worst joke. Instead, embrace the tranquility. Plan a cozy evening with some popcorn and a cheesy rom-com. Just make sure not to eat all the popcorn yourself, or you may find yourself in a sticky situation. Remember, the stars say it's all about balance—especially when it comes to sharing snacks.

Gemini, the social butterfly of the zodiac, your horoscope is throwing a party this week, and you're on the VIP list. However, before you RSVP with a resounding "yes," check your calendar. Juggling multiple commitments is your forte, but don't forget to schedule in some downtime. You don't want to be the person who flits from one event to another only to crash and burn halfway through the week. Enjoy the social scene, but also carve out some time to recharge. Netflix is calling, and the stars want you to answer.

For the more sensitive souls like Cancer and Scorpio, your horoscopes are all about emotional intelligence this week. Cancers, it's time to put your nurturing side to good use. Offer support to a colleague who's struggling, but don't let your empathetic heart turn into a crying sponge. And Scorpios, your horoscope warns against letting jealousy cloud your judgment. Remember, just because your work buddy got that promotion doesn't mean you should plot their demise. Instead, use that energy to focus on your own goals. The stars say teamwork makes the dream work, so keep it light and friendly.

As the week wraps up, remember that daily horoscopes can be your trusty sidekick in the roller coaster of business and personal relationships. They're not gospel, but they can provide a humorous lens through which to view the ups and downs of life. So, whether you're dodging a coworker's passive-aggressive post-it notes or navigating the complexities of a family dinner, let the stars guide you with a wink and a nudge. After all, in the grand scheme of the universe, we're all just trying to make it through the week without losing our minds—or our lunch.

Rituals and Routines: Aligning Your Life with the Stars

Rituals and routines are like the cosmic GPS guiding you through life's winding roads, and let's be honest, who doesn't need a little celestial navigation? Whether you're a meticulous Virgo or a free-spirited Sagittarius, aligning your daily habits with the stars can turn your mundane existence into a magical journey. Imagine waking up each day with the confidence of a Leo strutting into a room, knowing that your morning coffee ritual is not just caffeine; it's a sacred homage to the universe. So grab your astrological charts and get ready to sprinkle some stardust on your daily grind!

First things first, let's talk about those rituals. For instance, if you're a Cancer, you might find comfort in cocooning yourself in a blanket burrito while sipping herbal tea and plotting your next world domination strategy. Meanwhile, our fiery Aries friends could benefit from a morning workout that's more about channeling their inner warrior than actually breaking a sweat. The key here is to create rituals that resonate with your zodiac. They should feel as natural as a Gemini bouncing from one social event to the next, but with a little more structure—unless, of course, you thrive on chaos, in which case, carry on!

Now, routines are where the magic happens. Think of routines as the well-oiled machine that powers your daily life. For our meticulous Capricorns, this might look like a color-coded planner that would make even Marie Kondo weep with joy. On the other hand, a whimsical Pisces might prefer a more fluid approach, where routines are suggestions rather than mandates. The beauty lies in finding what works for you. If aligning your life with the stars means shaking things up every now and then, then by all means, throw in a spontaneous dance party in your living room. Just remember, even the stars have their own orbits!

Let's not forget the importance of aligning your rituals and routines with the lunar phases. Full moons are great for letting go and releasing toxic habits, while new moons are perfect for planting those ambitious seeds of intention. If you're feeling particularly adventurous, try timing your career goals with the astrological calendar. You might just find that your big presentation goes smoother than a smooth-talking Libra. Who knew that a little lunar love could turn your business meetings into celestial celebrations?

In the end, aligning your life with the stars is about more than just astrology; it's about creating a life that reflects who you are at your core. So go ahead, embrace your inner cosmic being! Whether you're channeling your inner Taurus with a love for all things indulgent or tapping into the analytical mind of a Scorpio, make those rituals and routines your own. Life's too short to follow someone else's roadmap when the universe has given you a personalized star chart. So gear up, get quirky, and let the cosmos be your guide!

When All Else Fails: The Art of Blaming Mercury in Retrograde

When life throws you curveballs, and your carefully laid plans go awry, it's time to whip out the ultimate scapegoat: Mercury in retrograde. This cosmic phenomenon, where the planet appears to move backward, is a favorite among those seeking a convenient excuse for everything from missed deadlines to awkward encounters at the office. Imagine blaming the communication breakdown with your colleague on Mercury's mischievous path instead of your own forgetfulness. Suddenly, you're not just a procrastinator; you're a victim of celestial shenanigans!

Picture this: you've sent an email that was supposed to seal the deal, only to find out it went to your cat's Instagram account instead. In the old days, you might have sheepishly owned up to it, but now, you can confidently proclaim, "It's Mercury retrograde! Blame the stars, not my typing skills!" This cosmic get-out-of-jail-free card allows you to shift the focus from your human blunders to the whims of the universe, all while your friends nod knowingly, having been there themselves.

In personal relationships, the allure of Mercury in retrograde becomes even stronger. Your partner forgets your anniversary? Well, obviously, Mercury's doing its backward dance! It's not that they're disorganized; they're just caught in the cosmic crossfire. This celestial reasoning can lead to a fascinating game of relationship blame, where every minor inconvenience becomes a chance to roll your eyes and say, "Seriously, do you even know what Mercury is doing right now?" It's a quirky way to lighten the mood when life gets a little too serious.

Of course, using Mercury in retrograde as a scapegoat isn't just about dodging responsibility; it's also about bonding with others who have been similarly affected by the cosmic chaos. You can gather with friends over wine, sharing your respective tales of woe: "I swear, my car wouldn't start because Mercury was retrograde!" This shared experience creates a unique camaraderie, allowing everyone to commiserate while secretly feeling relieved that they're not the only ones experiencing the planetary pandemonium.

Ultimately, while it's easy to default to blaming Mercury when things go south, it's also a reminder that life's little hiccups are part of the grand cosmic joke. Embracing the absurdity of it all can foster resilience, creativity, and a sense of humor in both business and personal relationships. So, the next time you find yourself in a pickle, just remember: it's probably not you; it's Mercury. And who wouldn't want to blame a planet for their problems?

Chapter 8: Final Thoughts: Should We Really Trust the Stars?

The Great Debate: Science vs. Astrology

In the grand arena of human understanding, two heavyweight contenders face off: science and astrology. On one side, we have science, armed with empirical data, rigorous methodologies, and a upbringing, and, yes, astrological influences. Use astrology as a conversation starter, not a personality contract. So when your colleague pulls out their zodiac chart to explain why they're late to the meeting, just nod knowingly and remind them that punctuality is a trait not exclusively reserved for Capricorns.

Next up, we need to talk about compatibility. Sure, your birth chart might suggest that you and your boss are like oil and water, but does that mean you should start job hunting? Not necessarily! Compatibility in astrology can provide insights, but it shouldn't serve as a relationship death sentence. Instead of avoiding the Taurus manager because they're "stubborn," consider harnessing their earthiness to ground your spontaneous ideas. It's like pairing peanut butter with pickles—not conventional, but you might just discover a surprisingly tasty combination.

Now, let's not forget that astrology can lead to some interesting conversations, but it's also essential to keep it light. If you find yourself in a heated debate about whether your best friend's Venus placement means they're destined to be single forever, it might be time to take a step back and breathe. Keep in mind that the universe is vast, and so are the possibilities for human relationships. Laughter is the best remedy for overly serious astrological analyses. So, when your friend starts explaining their latest astrological meltdown, just throw in a joke about how "even the stars can't help you text your crush back."

Finally, remember that astrology is just one lens through which to view ourselves and our relationships. It can provide insight, but it shouldn't be the sole basis for making business decisions or personal connections. Balance is key! Embrace astrology as an entertaining hobby that helps you understand the quirks of your colleagues and friends, but don't let it become an obsession. After all, the stars might influence us, but ultimately, we're the ones holding the steering wheel—hopefully without too many detours into cosmic chaos!

The Cosmic Conclusion: Embracing Your Birth Date Blueprint

As we wrap up this cosmic journey through the whimsical world of birth dates and personality traits, it's time to embrace your very own Birth Date Blueprint. Think of it as your astrological business card—except instead of a boring title and phone number, you get to showcase your unique quirks, strengths, and maybe even a few of those charming flaws. After all, who wouldn't want to introduce themselves at a networking event with, "Hi, I'm a Sagittarius with a penchant for daydreaming and a habit of stealing snacks from the office kitchen"?

Now, before you roll your eyes and mutter something about the zodiac being just a bunch of celestial mumbo jumbo, let's consider the undeniable truth: your birth date is basically the universe's way of giving you a cheat sheet for understanding yourself and others. Want to know why your coworker keeps stealing your lunch? Check their zodiac sign—maybe they're a Taurus, and that stubborn streak means they're just really devoted to lunch. Understanding these traits can help you navigate the minefield of office relationships without losing your sanity or your last slice of pizza.

Let's take a moment to appreciate the beauty of embracing our cosmic conclusions. When you start to view people through the lens of their birth dates, everything becomes a little more colorful. Suddenly, your overly ambitious Capricorn boss isn't just a workaholic; they're a driven individual with a penchant for spreadsheets and a secret love for motivational quotes. And your airy Gemini friend isn't just flaky; they're a vibrant social butterfly who thrives on variety. By recognizing these traits, you can cultivate relationships that are not only effective but also downright enjoyable—who knew that understanding zodiac signs could lead to fewer awkward silences and more harmonious collaborations?

Of course, navigating personalities in business and life isn't always smooth sailing. There will be clashes, misunderstandings, and moments when you'll want to throw your hands up and shout, "Why can't you just be normal?" But fear not! Armed with your Birth Date Blueprint, you can approach these challenges with a sense of humor. The next time your Virgo friend offers unsolicited advice about your messy desk, you can graciously remind them that chaos is just another form of creativity. After all, isn't that what life is about—finding joy in the quirks that make us human (and sometimes a little bit crazy)?

So, dear reader, as you step back into the world armed with your newfound wisdom, remember to wear your birth date as a badge of honor. Embrace the cosmic quirks that come with it, and use this knowledge to build bridges in both your business and personal relationships. Whether you're a fiery Aries charging ahead or a contemplative Pisces floating through life, your Birth Date Blueprint is your ticket to navigating the starry skies of human interaction. Now, go forth, shine bright, and may your relationships be as delightful as a perfectly timed punchline!

www.ingramcontent.com/pod-product-compliance
Lightning Source LLC
Chambersburg PA
CBHW070421230526
45471CB00006B/2912